Second Sleep

Susan Konz

cover image by Natalya Serebrennikova
www.natalyaserebrennikova.com

back cover photo by
Joyce DeFilippo

©-Copyright-Susan Konz-2016
©-Copyright-LION AUTUMN MUSIC PUBLISHING-2016
21 West 86th Street, Suite 807, New York, N.Y. 10024
U.S.A.
All Rights Reserved

*Imagine you are made of crystal
and someone ice picks you
and you shatter,
your cells coming
almost to despair
it is so good.*

-Ai

Foreword by Joyce DeFilippo

**

Untitled
Sunday Morning Hangover
How to Write a Bar Story
Poem about Leaving
Howie's Song
Desire # 2
to the bar
Who Died
Hangover #726
Twist Tie
Veal
Fire Safety
Unto the Dead there's No Geography
Desire # 3
Smoking Lesson
Bar Story
Prayer
Leslie
Desire # 4
Absolution
Red
Fox
Letting
Early
Dowsing
Shut Up about the Foxes
The Difference
Desire # 1
Boundary Effect
Time
A History in Four Parts or Persephone's Guilt
Dream # 26 with Consequences
Some Questions
August 28th
Totem

View from the Corner of the Bar
How to Listen to a Bar Story
Lleana
Holy Poem
Apology for an Ending
The Fight

I'm on a train back to Long Island at 2 am on a Wednesday, half-drunk and thinking about sleep. I've been living inside Susan's poetry for days, trying to write the foreword for this book. My phone is full of notes like "Incredible density of language!" and "How do we hold loss inside of our bodies?" and "What does it mean to desire something, to be desired?" and, though I am ashamed to admit it, "What the hell does the title mean?"

I have no idea what the title means. After almost 15 years of knowing Susan and after reading these poems backwards and forwards, I have no fucking clue. I realize that trying to decipher this in the early hours of the morning on the LIRR seems like a pointless endeavor, but that's what I'm doing. Scrolling through a PDF of the book on my phone, drifting in and out of delirium, I'm searching for signs of meaning. I'm listening to Cat Power on my headphones, pulled back into the past, a thing I do sometimes in an attempt to understand my own life in hindsight. We listened to these songs in Susan's childhood bedroom amidst our adolescent confusion, full of pain we couldn't articulate.

Looking back on it all these years later, the biggest difference between then and now is that we have finally broken through our own barriers of silence, silence we have had to deliberately unlearn, and we have gained the ability to tell our own stories. This book is about stories – stories that weave effortlessly between past and present, proving the past is never really dead, but always right underneath the surface as we make our best attempt to navigate the world. Also, apparently it has something to do with sleep.

When I think about sleep I think about dreams, how in dreams the past and present are always confounded, caught up in each other, almost inextricable. In dreams, those we have lost are still alive in some version of themselves, we are still fighting off people who have hurt us even if we are safe now, and we always seem to be stuck in some version of our childhood homes. In dreams we re-live our painful experiences again and again as if we could somehow do things differently, create a different outcome, win the fight against so many memories still unresolved. This book to me exists in the space between sleeping and waking – those few disoriented moments where you are coming back into awareness, trying desperately to hold on to that other world that exists only in the realm of dreams.

It's 2 am and I am trying very hard to stay awake by deliberating the meaning of the title *Second Sleep*. What it means to sleep… again. Maybe it's about existing in the fog of a half-conscious state, in a waking dream, never quite committing to one side or the other. Maybe it's about what cultivates that fog in us, what causes that dissociation, that disconnected way of moving through the world. Maybe it's about a second chance, a deliberate attempt to change the story by re-living, re-imagining, re-visioning. By articulating the story yourself this time around, being active instead of passive, giving yourself power in the telling. Maybe it's about a second life, a new way of being in the world that comes only after you move beyond the first. Maybe. I don't know.

When Susan told me the title she had decided on, I was too scared to tell her I didn't know what it meant. I figured after reading the book once or twice, the meaning would slowly reveal itself to me until I had the material for a brilliant meditation on the meaning of sleeping and waking and then sleeping again. Now, after struggling with it, I think it's okay to admit my ignorance. The book is most meaningful to me when I stop trying to analyze it. The narrative Susan has curated in this book is so strong, compelling, and brave. For me, the journey from beginning to end is a transformative experience of acknowledging the past, then emerging from an old way of living, learning a new way of seeing – the feeling of finally waking up.

—Joyce DeFilippo   April 2016

Second Sleep

Untitled

This is how it happened:
slow tick hands sculpt outline curves
my body   grey dust catches old
stained glass windowsill   that light is red
& yellow & green   there is a part
in this where I flood down to linoleum
floorboard cracks that don't hide
my mother   I am all forgiveness steel toe
combat boots clanging toes in frost
come inside it's warm   now beg
for it   the miracle of knowing
what good was it then? eyes
lolled back arms splayed   ripple
jolt   bop me right on the head Gideon
rip it out of me I am that woman
legs open but not indecent no in
the throes of salvation
salvation tether me my own body
dictator gypped and somewhere still
left me in a garden   trestles overhead are
grapes maybe twisting vines   there's
a soft breeze blowing in from the end
times   I am not cold I am not writing
the letter I do not take the call   at some
point my phone falls all together
into the ocean I am wading in & there's
no way to reach anyone and the trestles
shake & I am shapeless tripping down
into every way I learned hard hard &
safe this is how it happened: love turned sour
want got greedy I am all forgiveness
his hands carved that out in me

Sunday Morning Hangover

Glory, glory in the deadbeat hours of the morning.
Brick hymnals, the hands of the saved
have voices that march in harsh processional
toward August heat-wave Sunday sun.
Like wedding rice never come down,
they want to be that granular
shard piercing heaven – singular, many.
White needle thrown into the terrible
bright blue of god's glory.
One hundred plasterboard knees, cracked genuflection.
Ventriloquist enrobed in front fixes his voice
to the lord's lips and sings.

Me, here, worthless, unwitting spectator
with ears and eyes and nothing behind
crawl, Sunday Morning, as far as I can away
but know too the preacher's voice
calls me out. Lost lamb, I hearken wordless,
a low pulsing encased I offer up,
a heat in head, a syrup blood
thick, too sweet, been spoiled.
My sins made apparent on my flesh,
pale pink and pasty, red-rosed and psoriatic.
Taught long ago to know the pieces
of me that crumble off are the most hopeful.
They at least want to root themselves
in god's good dirt and reinvent,
diverge and be done with the heaviness of me.

Glory, glory for the saved.
Corner-cut hands clutch rosary.
Trees, sky, earth intact to suck
up their prayers, one more morning.
I call out to the black-robed preacher,
but he does not hearken back.
Never been hearkened to, me,
here where Sunday morning is
pouring bitter coffee

into lead sleep.
A body: fleshy, unwilling
in the impossible white
eye of the sun.

How to Write a Bar Story

Don't judge. Swim around other people's
murky water. Let yourself yellow fade and crisp with them

come down. I mean, go up first, way up because it hurts
to say everything is so precious because, fuck, everything

is so precious it pops live wire snaps at your tips; it frays
your hair singes golden spheres cycling in champagne

flutes, you down there, it hurts. Listen, come down,
look at this guy, three divorces a Stoli rocks moth

holes in his cardigan or her packing herself in ice with a book
doesn't need anyone – have a drink, have a few, roll that bite

around, learn how why not tastes. Let him call you
sweetheart, that's your knee under his hand. Let him slide

up your thigh high enough under the dirty oak lip of the bar
you don't feel it. This is your body, keep saying that. Develop

a taste for ryes. Tell the truth then laugh. Let him
take you home and when he's asleep

in the blue-blood dark pad through his house
barefoot, touch his things softly. They exist.

His maid will come remove your traces after, I tried
to fuck her too, he'll tell you. Know what you are. All these

lives, a jade jewelry box on the nightstand,
a papier-mâché cube, a bent corkscrew,

a gold watch, broken clasp. Hold them quick when no
one sees, you're nobody, just listen, it happened, it's real, you

remember, it hurts, you're nobody,
pour thirteen shots, it's important, let it all go

fuzzy – hold everything you see,
palm it, it's here, it's precious,

it's so fucking precious somewhere between novelty
and import like he says that Sunday morning coming

in it's going to be a long day, Sue, crack
an egg in my beer. Didn't they use to do that?

Poem about Leaving

This is an old question. My mother
standing across the table half-listening.
Her hands wrist high in flour, bent toward
the mess of it – yolk and bread crumb,
pale eerie chicken breast.

I omitted the kiss, how his hand traced
the seam of my bra, tugged at the jutting
wire but asked her what to do
with him. All my electric sixteen

years magnetized in the wrong
directions. She said stay. She said love
accepts. Love stays.

Did she already know the plod and lull
of the trains? How leaving gets old
that way, but feels inevitable

now. I have accepted a lot.
All of it with my hands.
And when I left you for the last
time, I ran down your stairs and tripped
along your stoop – I had to.

Your big dumb wet eyes were too sincere
& wanting. It's pulse run in me stay stay stay,
but now all I can do is –

outside the theater, in his mother's living
room, I walk away. Right out from bed sheets.
Once is hard but she'd never guess how easy

it gets. Still smelling him on me as I board the train.
This is an old question. My mother ironing
her husband's slacks every morning.
Rising early, kettle on the stove. Running

her fingers along the perfect creases.
Later, frying the chicken with lemon
and herbs. Some recipe I never
bothered to learn.

Howie's Song

In the corner he shoots
    insulin into his gut
before shaking

his glass in the air,
    neat and ya know,
full.

It's really,
    you wouldn't guess, but
it's really very easy

he says, and he frowns
    then iron presses himself &
he's back to first thing's

first. Howie let's sober you up & then
    oh what's the point?
It's aborted out there – static,

mid-moment, sun crashing down the tops
    of mid-sized sedans
for ever & ever &

anyway I'm starting
    to have your memories.
Those girls at Grace's so sweet

& lolli-licked & ready –
    just trying to make a buck.
Just to touch

the pale pink lace
    pig-tailed at the tits.
Those poor girls,

Howie, what fun.
    That one time
we held a gun

to our friend Nick's head
    & cocked it
for the feel. The stupid

bastard really got
    terrified. I'm swimming,
Howie, in the in-ground

pools of nouveau-riche
    cocaine dealers. I'm dancing until
the oxycontin kicks in

and then we're flying.
    I'm giving
my wife her black eye,

or I'm the woman cowering
    below you, Howie,
I think I'm the space

between your fist
    & her patient skin. I think
I remember

there being something
    else before this, outside here:
something simple, something

you didn't need to ask for,
    something necessary.

Desire #2

Try that first kiss you bent and curved into
me the way a kid goes to gum a candy apple
and I'll not break my cower. See, there's

this hot white windmill that pops (that pop!) at my center
and sunspots and kneels me. I am tired of hashing
out other people's anger. Give me the old cigar boxes
filled with my grandmother's jewelry. I want

the peppermint patties she gave my brother, that
sweet, that bite. I want the turtle green and beehive yellow,
her plastic pearls. My hands in those boxes. I want
to let this album play on repeat all night. I want

your want. Tiramisu in small crystal
bowls with copper spoons. Fresh cranberries
to suck & grass to spit the seeds into. I want
my feet hot, naked on black tar. I want suburban
paranoia, the bored rumors of ageless widows
with their small white poodles. I want to be invited

over for bridge to count the cards & chip
the deck & hear them say my mother
was a whore maybe as a teenager or her skirts
too short. That she came home drunk & peed
in the bushes. I want to be despised by the
rosary altar society; to be the laugh my mother
is trying to hide in church.

I want the raspberry ice cream pops my friends
gave me after her funeral (this is too much)
they are melted & all I remember
some man across a phone *I can help
you* – let me tell you exactly when I stopped
believing in whatever redemption is. Let me

try the first time: red Swedish fish
on the sidewalk candy kiss & too much tongue, two
black bruises on my neck. My mother
too prudent even to punish me. This is so
indecent. Let me light your smoke instead
& you can invite yourself to dinner. I'll burn the roast
and we can fuck in the baster or we can work on finding
god again together. It's just that it's been all this time
& I'm just trying to tell you

one time something bad happened, one time
a woman flung out a white linen tablecloth
in the blue light of the restaurant to set & it
was raining & night & how beautiful it wilted
down & laid itself flat. The wind is like this
& cold. It gets in the middle of you & won't go.

to the bar

and the buses are outlaws
reckless blue streaks inconsiderately
barreling me through patchwork bare
tree limbs and pavement. Potholes,
landmines that send us flying up from our seats,
crashing down in this plasticine war
where no one ever really dies.
I am listening to Irish folk songs,
hymns, why not, in my father's voice
had he ever opened his mouth
to reconstruct those confessions.
Indented strip malls, sturdy sidewalks,
good for holding you up in the long night.
The kids stub their cigarettes against
the street side, getting grey dust and
gypsum on their fingertips.
The gas station attendants are my brothers
slouched and paranoid microcosm James Dean's
without the hair, smoking in furious blasts
before boss comes back or all
the petrol pumped underground
becomes nothing but carbon dioxide and heat.
Birds are my mother, perched and dauntless
or, no, my mother is the sun – glorious
and impossibly far. Dying or already dead,
swelling before she bursts. And I am alone,
or fugitive, or hiding, passively defying
the speed limit in my sloped seat.
And when I step down I will drink
glass after glass of holy wine and pray
to St. Jude that I not be forgotten
by dead Irishmen who don't want to
stop singing, and who could blame them,
their words the only thing beyond the reach
of the unforgiving landscape.

Who Died

Who was split like two lips
peeled apart on the Ford's silver grill.
The deer she carried this way for fifteen
feet still alive & going scarlet. Its
hind legs kicking, scratching the hood.

This is your story told over the dirty
high top. Your evil stepmother cracked
in half on some endless country road at night.
About how she wanted to stop the sight,
the impossible black of one open eye
but the paramedics came instead

for her and not the deer. Weeping
and mewing like a child right there
for god to see with his one sleeping eye
blinked open. Maybe the guilt, you say, another life
she destroyed & I agree it must have been truly
terrible but can't image her envy. To see
who gets to be absolved by sectioning, halved
and allowed to be emptied of everything
carried inside.

Hangover #726

I am plagued by the coffee
I don't want to drink.
Daylight; catastrophe.

Out the door
the street's awake
& jangling & me

heavy cloud headed
my dumb dead
eyes slicking

around half-lidded.
I wasn't born
like this. Shut

up, shut flower
wanting
to de-pollinate.

I step out.
Want the earth
to slurp me

back inside
I can imagine
the feel

of the good dirt.
These are my
father's eyes

I want
to make
a return.

At least
my cab driver
is also suicidal.

When my cheek
slapped the plastic
divide I knew

I could never
keep you.
You don't hit

hard enough.
And who could love
a thing like this?

Dumb dog
laid out
for the kicking.

Twist Tie

I keep wrapped around my finger –
Remember. I remember. I've made a promise
to remember. Some godheard prayer, I'm sure. I'm

desperate honestly. Everything comes to me in slashes
now like the sunset through blinds at dinner
after summer little league. My mother up mid-meal
to pull the still life curtains shut. Everything

smelt of fresh cut grass then & watching sprinkles spark
on. I'm grateful how steeled so young I was against
the table shaking as my father carved roast
beef I'd only poke at. I couldn't stop but think of those cows

upstate walking dumb across the road just beyond the sign
CattleXing. They Xed and we waited, what a sight
my huffing father, my mother gawking at the mute heft
of nature. Of course, the whole parade
just brute lugging across concrete - so easy away from
whatever shouts behind them. My two brothers, caesars, asleep
behind me. If I couldn't bite that how could I bite this. I,

even then, had trouble with difference. The past
two days now I've worn this twist tie around my middle finger
I swivel thoughtlessly. It's garbage.

My protest against ending, keeping this, mine
to turn. I'm telling you, I can make it harder,
turn it up or down. It's here,
like me. Something I say I get to choose
when it stays, how it goes.

Veal

Green socks with no-slip rubber grip
poking out off white bedsheets. Two feet
bobbing nervously, little boy feet. Feet
that did something wrong and know it.
My father's hospital gown open in the back slips
off his shoulder when he reaches down to pull up
the bedsheet. Trauma room. Wheeled between blue
curtains. *That guy over there wasn't doin'
too good.* Behind the blue

is nothing: no bed, no nurse, no patient, no
table. Boyish lying down, I've never talked
to him this way. His bottom lip a little purple,
a little red, scratched at, swollen. *They use
those on you?* some silver orbs hover
above the bed. *Not yet*

Fluorescent flickering smell will stick on him for days. He
calls me Sue and complains about the food until I promise
to bring him dinner. It's winter. It's turning over
clockwork grief into anger. I'm a pebble rolling along the
lip. I'm slipping, quiet. It's icy then warm in the
restaurant. I order spaghetti and veal and a glass
of cabernet while I sit and wait & want the owner
to fall in love with me – my coat tied at my waist, my
windblown hair, my big brown eyes, my dying father – look

how everything erodes. Look how much water
has passed through this place & gutted
it. The hospital is too sharp and insistent after
the wine, I drop off the meal and kiss his bloated
cheek. Everything about me is a little off center
but I'm the only one left who will come to him,
bring him the poor veal in Styrofoam & wish him good
night. I can't think of him in all that light all night long
how unbearable, how clearly he can see the half eaten
meat, terrible flat and grey even after he closes the lid.

Fire Safety

Touch the doorknob: if hot, do not open.
Better to let one room burn than singe
yourself. If singed stop, drop and roll.
Keep rolling until down the block at the neighbor's
house you used to call Aunt Barbara who
has made you cookies. Eat the cookies.
Wipe away the crumbles like rubble, sift
through and find the fallen chocolate chip.
Eat the chocolate chip but do not let her
see this. When finished say, "Thank you
Aunt Barbara," and keep rolling.
On Thanksgiving when your widowed
father burns the turkey and the oil catches
fire in the oven, do not throw water
around the turkey. Do not weep or try
to roll to a more functional kitchen.
Talk calmly while the flames lap the green
and white ceramic tiles your mother laid
until you remember that it's baking soda
you need. Find the baking soda above
the burning oven and dispense.
Never fix the oven.
Leave that for the terrible real
estate agent with the dyed blonde
permanent up-do and blue eyeshadow
from 1986 who will come to list your mother's
house once your father has turned all the savings
into handles of vodka and ash. Vodka is very
flammable. By the transitive property your
father is very flammable. You've always suspected
this but now you know – do not spark anything
in his presence. If he starts to smoke, push him
to the ground and roll him for as long as is reasonable
or until safety is established. Safety is key. When
your brother lights his left leg aflame with zippo
refills and a cigarette, do not believe the doctors
when they tell you it is not fatal. The fever
he contracts will be a different kind of fire.

Roll him to the hospital and give the people
there all your money. Use credit cards and payment
plans and sometimes running from the waiting
room mid-sentence. Every night, touch his forehead,
if hot, remain vigilant. Do not let him burn.

Unto the Dead There's No Geography

Cigar smoke follows a pathway of vents in mid-January
your husband puffing away, all the windows up tight against
the cold. Your body smalling, just un-making itself,
unable to fill Sunday's floral skirts and church shoes.
I kept myself busy with routes to doctors, from clinicians
with your scripts. I cooked you lentil soups and chilis,
and when you couldn't eat those things, lettuce with oil
and red wine vinegar, the salt crushed between my fingers.
I was so angry at your body for not knowing what it needed,
I thought I would never soften. I started to feminize
the ambrosia of your blood's rotten cells, the intricate,
impossible pathways they carried and now I've given up

on beauty. I can only draw straight lines from place
to place. I have no imagination left – even in my dreams
you are dead or half dead or almost or sort of –
I drove across a country to escape how dead you had gotten.
I smashed your husband's camera in Albuquerque
and hid in basketball courts watching teenage boys pass
around a fifth of Georgi vodka. I looked for signs of you
in crags of rock in the Mojave and when I found none
got myself dizzy enough in Amarillo to talk to the cowboys
who didn't need to hear your story, but mostly just moving
to move – one thousand two hundred and fifteen miles
of interstate forty – giving myself land and sky and waiting
for you to show me you were right. You spent your whole life
believing death was a doorway you could wave from the other
side of, but I am finding it every day like cigar smoke
sticking in your clothes, your hair,
you can't shake the stink of it.

Desire #3

       Let this be about dried out flowers
in asphalt puddles waiting heavy
with meaning like she's here or
she's not gone too far or if you listen
you can hear some angel whisper
her song up in the fifteenth octave, you know,

       what the blue haired Catholic ladies say.
And let this be about them: how kind
they are and stuck behind a tray of baked
ziti for the boys, balancing a cheese basket
on their heads *we're so sorry for your*
loss. Remember where it broke where

       you couldn't feel any more empathy
for their silver satin empathy and you got
bad, got bent and where go then?
There are highways for people like you, yeah,
be a boy and find some hard to hide behind. Go
ahead blame it on men as the long way
to blaming it on being a woman,
a woman like your own mother. Stop feeling

       songs in your knuckle twitch. Be numb
to film and art and kissing. Get scared,
say nothing. Go empty like girls on cabbage
diets. Float pale green in the cloudy water
like that. Eat the sun & wash it down
with dust. Never turn down a party. Let
resentment build up like the forts you made with

       your brothers from twigs and wet dirt
when no one sees your stratosphering
absence. You're good at it.
You learned from her quiet

& hitching but please don't realize your own
complicity until years later. Then be left
with her flowers purple gone auburn
and held by a ribbon come from
someone forgotten. Wait now for

    flash fence to topple, all edges meld. Maybe joy
didn't die it just went disco bowling two dollar
Tuesdays at Tully Lanes. It makes sense to
seek what hurts you most. Tattoo your forearms
lilac. Be the kind of girl to jump off the bay bridge
stoned, assumptive.

    Open your mouth, Hail Mary
mother grace who art in the attic.
Remember the meter of worship, those beads
between your fingers angry, alive.
Remember how everything shimmers this way,
shouts up ecstatic, hungry.

Smoking Lesson

Not suffocating, that metallic taste
caught in the back of your throat. And how
choking we didn't stop. Unremarkable,
I guess. Not hidden but tread over:
the dark then light. Sun, tire. Bike's
swish overhead – the electric flash of the L
train before we knew that rattle. And you,
not old enough, not cruel, but wanted me
to do it right – held the lit one to my lips –
said breathe – in – now, again – not

like my father's smoking – ash soaked
and musted, we were fresh from rolled-up
jeans in the tide. Our breath still red &
sweet from boardwalk candy. Your hands
limber, acrobatic as you grabbed my shoulder
and laughed. Not like that.

Like this.

Bar Story

This guy here knows a guy whose friend just
turned yellow one day like his skin was paper
left out in the sun. His liver was leaking, it turns out
so the doctors, they patched him up – this is how the guy
says it and he was fine, the friend was. I even saw him some
time later that week behind a dewars and water, he waved
over the glass to me and I don't think he's asking to die
at all but he's certainly entertaining the question.
Either way this guy here says the guy's like invincible,
he'll probably never die and really, wouldn't that just
be the goddamn truth – that this guy will outlive all of us
who are batting death around like it's a ball
of tinfoil anyway – half wanting the catch but mostly
just enjoying how it's always a breath away
but never quite. On the corner
of the block I grew up on there was a lady
who I remember for all the ambulances
that came when I was six and my mother
maybe too startled to remember who she was
talking to told me how she had slit her wrists
and locked herself in the garage with the Cadillac running
and how, she said, my mother did, that she really wanted to die
like she wasn't fucking around and she seemed to really
respect that about this woman whose house
was subsequently cleaned out by some son
of hers who none of us knew who came up
from Florida or Jersey or god knows where
and took away anything we would recognize
so that the house could be sold to some other
couple and the rest of us could get on and finish
forgetting her completely.

Prayer

Oh Lord, if I'm lying,
        strike me down.
It's been too long &

        I have tried
to disembroider myself
        from these blanket

sins. All my soft
        nos are screaming
yes and I left

        some man I love
in a barroom downtown
        Oh, Lord, I'm lying

strike me
        down.
Don't just leave me here

        in this gypsy cab
refusing to go
        stuck behind a city bus

in midtown traffic.
        Don't forget me
to my own sins.

        Make my vices
business expenses.
        Deduct me, Oh Lord,

I didn't mean it
        or I didn't know
what I meant –

                what difference then –
Punish me
        by dulling me

to the stories
        make me forget
how they kept me

        alive (why leave me
words enough
        to drivel on?)

Or take, instead, away
        all the soft edges
of sad & leave me

        the burnt point
of anger, Lord,
        I can only see myself

through another's eyes –
        in your blinking
absence I've turned

        to other fathers, Father,
why make me
        a will so bold

and this temperance
        so weak?
Why born in me

        this want of absolution
then you run off,
        then you hide, too?

Leslie

I should have killed that bitch
he said. Choked her with my own hands
Then demonstrates my body how he would have
and laughs What was your name again? Leslie?

Why not – I've never seen her sturdy legs in dark
denim, suede boot below the knee walking intentional
from the courthouse door, wide-gait. A body
that skis in Vermont with second-husband Randy
a body that gets ventilated, sweat out & spa-ed

A litigious body Leslie still alive & me
her proxy for this anger. I've lost mass or
is it density. I'm something now a hand
can pass through, some drawn spook.

It's fine. Most of the time I don't even know
when I'm lying anymore to be honest.
Don't say that. You shouldn't
say that I told him. At night, alone, I trace my hands
over my body under blankets like even in all that dark
I still can't look and it's unfamiliar – rubbery & expanding
I squeeze the fat at my hips, finger the purple-gashed
skin, carry my breasts, my belly I've been feeding flexi
straws and the silver halide off old photos and still
I'm surprised when I come to him hungry. When

he says I wanted to but I didn't that's the difference.
To be honest when he said *out to see* I pictured a hay
colored skiff, some forgotten thing bobbing in blue.

This body won't take
anymore. I mean, nothing holds
& how can I know it's there?
The thing he feels at the end of his fingers.
Those warm hands at my throat.

Desire #4

What's mine is big enough to swallow
me whole. Two-for-one up the road martinis
& buy-one-try-one tapas if you have a lover – I think
that's what they're saying. It's primordial

how I'm being sold. The flashing neon bar signs
like some outdated noir with dead detective.
My flat-footed voice is calling murder & no takesies-
backsies but it's only a whimper, I'm deluded,

everything green's been replaced by flat &
there's no color in that. It's all fable anyway,
the green – some Irish countryside, some
mossy bough. I hear of it but can't imagine

how far – I've grown
intractable, some snake trying to height myself
in pencil lead against the white basement pillar
but always being shot at, harpoon dodging &

for what? And how am I still wrapped up in myself?
That snake eating its own tail always ending
& beginning and eternally not going any
where – come on. I'll burn down
the house with incense sticks. I'll de-collarbone
myself and play Yahtzee with the shrapnel. I'll
give my goal to know my height. Something

certain, something I can hold. The ending –
the certain promise like Hamlet's poison tip
and Adam's apple-mouth. I think I hear too
sometimes Greek in this suburban sea. It sounds like gulls
kamikaze onto jetties. Something triadic
in the smattering crash. Maybe your waters are my
waters. Maybe Job & John are having tea on
desert rock formations. Ayahuasca in the pencil-thin
night. If all love is madness than the rabid are the seekers.

I close my eyes to them & breathe in Irish
countryside, the South of Wales, some fabled
green I dive down to end in.

(absolution)

I dream he's next to me in seagull sounds
The air is pulling out to sea, tastes like salt
I'm lost. He's not mine –

It doesn't matter
some daughter telling me
I'm slipping – no
this is not what she says,
she says, It doesn't matter
we just need

to get home, but I've forgotten
topography, landmarks fade on sight –
the azaleas outside my mother's house are dripping

pink. The corner mailbox bluing as she
fades & I can't help when he comes plotting
me, giving me details on how we'll hide what we've done.

What we've done is something to do with cracking
eggs in the dark, has to do with deshelling. Signs
are flashing –

nonstop violence
all night free
I'm wide awake
it's morning. I'm listening
to the phone ring, but won't answer
I'm trying to weigh a wrong
done with half a heart

He's walking now ahead of me,
bowlegged like my father both
knees cocked back unbending

he's lilting
as I'm fingering the stones
incanting to the pure
all things are pure,
but there's no give. He takes
my arm and squeezes tight

This will leave
a mark he says something
you can be sure of.

Red

Aberrant and sunny, I'm out in a Cherokee
red that does not belong to me
slouched like I think cowboys slouch
against the *encomienda's* log fences. Watching
the children play bocce ball in the sloped grass.
I am trying with the word family
to feel the same blood coursing
and know what I know that I am bound
to things tightly like green of grass
and blare of sunlight and red
that beats against my eye
lid when it is too bright:
I have feared you inside of me
plotted murders against progeny & will
if must. Your heart sounds the same as mine
and its – pathetic knocking
against something dull, pink and fleshy.

Fox

boughs slitched down
as burdens snapped to bend
the earth

accepts this
and him
dancing somehow tip-toed
though thick-limbed
and bottom heavy between

what's left of branches
behind her tent
where she sings
to her little fire
her song

she stitched together from
milkweed blooms and cigarette butts
this whatever she can

find song
keeps her
warm but fox

takes invitation
to dance her
to sleep

not seeing her sly
now and fast braiding
the thick grass into tethers

and whistles
what she's learned

one good note
to rattle the pollynoses
and syphon dew

from moss over maple trees
she'll bite down hard

and spit into the stinkweed
what she's learned

by mouth
not to trust
and pick up tent

if she must
to leave him
wandering in forsythia
and upsetting the bees
while she casts
out into
salivating waters

Early

Sun downing pale yellow slats through Venetian
blinds. She's on the floor & spinning herself with bare
feet, toes spread, knees bent. Her back fulcrum to shape
of isomers, diadems on the cold speck tile. This is early
in the story before words hold shape and thud down like
sleep like *please* like *in there* like *early*. It's early & twinning.
There's still time before her parents call her down to supper.
There's London broil & brown gravy. She won't say anything about
the moment after great pain
when small things snap and crystalize. So she latchkeys
to the light tree-broken along the ceiling – it's useful. Mouth full
of potato and salt and each young foot slid into Sunday tights her little body
red meat & not her own. It's useful to know what is salvation made as small
as it gets. A pocket thing hid early, still wet & tastes like no.

Letting

The cops came for the shouting
then just stood around your kitchen
knocking into the holiday mugs

you tell me. Your father and stepmother
got them called third time this week for
throwing the plates, some drunk swash
of night between them. That's why
you're here bouncing from foot to foot
on the cold slush street. Your breath
visible and smelling like vodka & the fake

cherry off maraschinos. Some time before
this a man folded up and handed me a paper
with a date from my past on it. He knew
something I didn't want to know myself
he told me. He had my memories & wanted
to make out across the center console. I was
listening to the car's heat whistle & it's bullshit
that he might see with some infrared eye
where and why pain springs, but I remember

letting myself believe I was letting myself
believe and I don't know why except that I
am no good as a mystic unless I'm half dead
like all the good ones. That's why I let you

finish your story & I don't ask much & laugh
with you about the shouting and about later
when it's about your father passed out
in the turnpike's grassy median just starting

to freeze. His two dogs roaming now & already
given up on him letting himself sink
right down into it braver than whatever
is there to see.

Dowsing

Barrow blasted and bent over the lip
separating the strawberry plants from grass
and wild onion.

The backyard where my grandfather picks up
a forked twig fallen from the oak tree. His hands shingled
and veining

He says it will tip down where there's water below,
he's deliberate – teeter and straighten. I watch him
from the slab of sunlight

on concrete just behind: brown slacks, grey penny loafers
circling the yard. *This is how we used to do it* he says.
It's early summer.

He hands me the oak, shakes my shoulder to loosen my grip.
I follow its pointed shadow along the ground. Walk steady,
transfixed.

I'll learn later that this is a kind of witching in the wet soil. This asking
toward the burrowing worms, but here I am soft sun my
shoulder, my toes laced
with sharp green grass

and for that, the floods. After we found the water main my grandfather,
slacks rolled above the ankles, wading in the pooling basement.
Him & my father

in their 12th street apartment up to their waists in the muddy stuff
(how it got up the high rise I'll never know). Then back again
submerged
alone in my mother's kitchen

watching the sun rising, sitting away from the table
fish-tanked, impossible. But for now he tells me not to move it
just let it be moved. It's delicate

how we want what we want from any hand that offers
& my grandfather, pockmarked diviner, how much of it did he already know?
Who or what pulls the branch toward the soil saying

here, *here*, *here*?

Shut Up about the Foxes

He talks suicide then rolls an uneven joint against my living room table &
I'm not sure how much of it I believe – hear myself saying maybe you are alone,
maybe you're not wrong and it's not bad maybe the trick is to not rail against it

after all I've already left the pop & crush of anxiety on the drive to the show. I can
turn numb once I'm there it's been so long, how have you been, it's been too long, too long &
something else I forget. I came to see her play. Am in love at her lonely & how she hits it
quiet. I don't think they see when the guitar string snaps and it's the shaking before almost

tears. That day Margaret cut my hair hungover from beer flights without blow & confesses
a love of North American wildlife – artic wolves and Canadian foxes.
You would never guess right? She's shaky and sleeved neck down in ink, Roman
numerals down her throat in red counting what I don't know, no, I wouldn't have,
but her wife is tired, she says, of hearing about it – the animals – stage left, Britney nods

and rolls her eyes – everyday. I bring my brother salmon and potatoes that ride
in the passenger seat with the music too loud to keep up, and he is every day smaller
and folding into the purple bedsheet he wears. A Roman emperor if not for the internal hemorrhaging that pools scarlet below the
rib God took out like a secret, like the pouch
that holds I don't want to anymore. I was trying to fly, he says & did

he says and wanted that broken when the concrete ascended like a promise. And Krishna,
I don't think, said anything about legumes, which to eat, which are sacred – probably all –
but I listen to the man in the parking lot that night go on about how his chakras are just so &

On the causeway the flares burn nothing – semicircling grey asphalt – I slow
and swerve for whatever needed protecting before. And now my own voice, I hear it, sounds angry,
rollicks and I want it to shut up, to shut up about the ache & lull, shut up about the beauty & horror
I am justifying alone to a boy I will send home sad & high. I'm not indifferent, but I want to be, bully, boy, it's all down when you're looking down.

The Difference

He grabs the lip of the bar, pounds the surface,
250 exactly after that last field goal. Pay up.
It's funny. It's fun, loud. God,

I've got to get out of here. He takes me down
to the water & it's good because it doesn't belong
to anyone, but he makes it a gift he gives me

with his gnarled right hand on my shoulder.
I'm a little girl if he says so. I'm safe now he's
stopped what he might do. What he might do

always mostly in the eyes, thick black
rims and snarl to the lip attending when
no one sees. I might be losing

my mind with all these things I can never say.
They are too simple. Show how I am
simple. It's brilliant

how big he's gotten being gone. How I hand him
the stuff of my life: a knotted teal necklace, some
dried out hyacinth blossoms and let him return them changed.

He's no storyteller.
Too sweeping in the snag
his net catches. Why do I let him collect?

When will I give myself permission to walk out into that water,
bear the unowned salt, find my body outline magnified
her waves, let those gulls sound my story crashing
against the browned jetties or those impossible fish –

I'm one of them if I want.

I've the whole thing to dive into if I want.

Desire #1

Some crab trapped in some heartless
net, its pincers snipping out
but cannot break free. Cunning
that way how he holds back – some
wormy guilt edging in that makes him
soft – rejects the snap of it, the bite of
I want that I want you I want –

All signal to the blinking eye – the turn
away but glancing back. Desire
is thorny and tasteless. It jabs & interrogates
my body bent & pushed. Before I was a woman
I was something to investigate, prod &
pluck – some turnip from some hearty soil –
produce me then scurry off. His desire is
crab snap – awkward & hungry &
all at once blind to the name
on its tongue.

Boundary Effect

There's something in my periphery.
Smoking on the stoop, my brother's head
spins somehow completely around, baseball cap
falling off in the severance. I'm sure, I see

it clear as morning & don't question, let the calm
overtake me when this happens. I've cauled my fear
so I don't jump, so nothing surprises me,
so I don't even bend to retrieve the hat

because look! Look at me! I'm safe, finally,
after all that kvetching & it's no big deal
anymore. I can move beyond these bad dreams
that spin around, surface and undertow me, can

hold my tongue before the scream to see if his head
sits right when he lights his next cigarette, wait to decide
it's nothing even when I recognize these things dying
around me – a spastic moth in the forty watt

porch light, a rabbit three counties north, mid-lane
who won't even blink as I'm coming straight
toward him and why won't he move if he's
more animal than me, more programmed

to exist. Maybe I'm the one frozen, scared, half-
way to meet my family where highways have no
streetlights. I tried, but couldn't swerve
fast enough. I'm left angry to be the one

to have to remember the thump-thump
the tires made and how somehow I'm allowed
to, made to keep driving, while he got to blink
and cease, no kvetching about fairness,

about not sleeping, eyes & cheeks flying off
into corners, half in dreams, not meaning it, never
meaning it, but cagey from the start it keeps giving me
like the flicker when walking into a room knowing I came

with a purpose, but unable to recall it. My life beginning
to become this moment, turning around and again
in the kitchen, garage, closet, hallway, new
to myself, my things, absent of all

memory but one, and even then, only half fleshed out,
something to be discerned about me, this somehow that
I am bound to my surroundings, how I'm sure I can't
leave until I know what called me in.

Time

        Five o'clock is panting, humid until you come.
I'm waiting in 700 different outfits each
uncomfortable, flicking cigarettes into coffee for the prediction

of the ash. It takes time,
but everything reveals itself this way.
I'm in your bed surrounded by empty bottles and trash
where I stay safe, safe about 16 centuries

since you left for work & I'm watching my sons
have daughters and those girls puff gray smoke
out from between their lips, sitting on my mother's stoop
leaning away from the obscenity of their round bellies.

What I'm trying to say there have been
hundreds before me and will be millions after and we're all waiting
for you to appear in the doorway, throw your jacket over the
coatrack and pause there framed for the reveal – today's news
fifteen dogs set free in the shop, three terrible mothers
harassed you, 22 dollars went missing
from the registers. Do you know how much

I love you? A thousand years of salt and buttered toast,
two decades preparing, 900 days before you said hello,
415 hours locked in the bathroom, you screaming, you tyrant,
can't you see I'm sick? I'm trying to say
we went back too far. I'm Penelope without
virtue & spent now.

How boring each day I bent to pick up your jacket
hang it right
on the rack. Do you know how much I love you?
I've done time in other men's beds, rolled their pillow down
into tiny dolls, our children,
        our fantastic children. I'm fast
now and free from you after all this time
I've forgotten how routine keeps warm, how love
builds castles, waits.

A History in Four Parts
or Persephone's Guilt

one

I dreamt you dark
and neon pink.
I burrowed to yr chest.

You were sage & kind
the way you are
only in absence,

but what ached after
was the memory of night
in your attic room,

wrapped in your fear,
my ear to your heart
where *it's okay,*

it's okay. Your song
rocking me away
never could stop

that silver fish
from slipping into
my blood stream,

drawn to the rot
at the tamped, safe
center point of us.

two

I am watching myself watch nothing,
waiting for history to swoop down
& fill me up with all the people I've been.

Persephone taken down, I get –
how pallid the wildflowers her hand let drop.
Big-eyed and hungry down there –

Persephone, voiceless, save a song lilting below
the dirt, so faint only the sun caught it.
It not meant for anyone, really.

It no plea, more lament –
It sifting through my dirge here
where only in my memories I am so quiet,

stock still and caught, bent to the day glow
sun: *I'm so sorry. I miss you.* I still remember
the pang of those seeds you'd feed me –

red and sour.

three

Because I had to eat, I had to stay.
This rule now divides my time.
If I return to you,

like some spelunker through all this gore,
I return to my affections. Promise me
they haven't shriveled.

I'm rife with rotten second chances.
Filthy from snooze buttons at the foot
of every bed

Is it my fault I was born into sleep?
A heritage of dreams without antecedent,
did I choose this?

I'm too hungry these days to think.
What else could I have done?
You're angry,

but I'm sick, fast burning out, away
from the damp palm of our
sleepy love.

four

I don't have a good tie for this –
you sitting next to me on the old rug,
wax sealed and coffee stained,

the television in your mouth flashing
blue and human shapes that splash
against the false wood paneling –

I've wronged you and maybe you know.
I wanted to see the blue dome above
the dirt, got tired of being your lover

in hell. Even though it was so good,
your sweet voice shaking the linoleum,
sneaking through the streets at night

like kids. Sneakers off, skipping over dirt
and glass. Your eyes dancing, not seeing
me, the grey suburban night –

You, deep in your own mind, holding out
your hand for me to take. For me to never
have to be alone.

All I ever needed to do
was follow you
all the way down.

Dream # 26 with Consequences

My mother's a wart, a wiped out baby swaddled
by zombied dads and petrified second cousin Peter's
mauled right hand, asking for sweet port in aperitif
crystal but no one's coming – when the funeral starts,

there in the box rolling over and threatening to tip off
the boards with my mother, a baby gauzed in purple in my
arms. She isn't dead is
refusing death like a tray of jerk shrimp at a
wedding reception so

Dad does what he has to do like he would
and goes to find something blunt
and hefty to clobber her
with because otherwise
she'll fuck up the funeral
he says, and he's right,
what will the guests do?

They're hungry and mostly
still alive so they've got that over us &
demand the respect the living demand
from the dead.

So dad's trying and bless him, Peter with his gnashed
up car-body, brother Mike, brother Paul come grunged &
high and they're all trying to get her still
in the mange of the party all
while keeping a polite arms length presence –

a lot of whisped names in open window breezes and
cabinet doors that swing open and stay
that way all night and wait
for the living to come get oatmeal
from the microwaveable packets above
the counter and see them open and know we're here –

out of respect this is done. This customary thing &
the guests are so grateful they hardly notice
the duck and pivot of my thirsty mother

right out from my arms and headed
god knows where.

Some Questions

after Dylan Thomas

Why fret what the blood says this October?
Why worry if the stars whistle Dixie
If the pallid beach cries uncle? The wind
does what it wants. The raven, if you listened
coughs from loneliness. The dumb
grey sky just goes on without offering.

**

Where are you – shut & out there on the terrace?
Walking along some nighttime bridge? Look
at them – the women in their holiday reds,
the children all treble and vibration. They
are spelling things out for you – some memory,
some starry chick forgotten in dirty linens,
some dusty father fingers round a lip
of whiskey. So grateful, be so grateful for their shapes
that lilt and lift and rise.

**

Let's let the sun rise. Let's make it
glorious and daytime. I have promises to make
to the coming-up sun. I have proclamations
to regret to the dew & the birds perched
on naked boughs. What time is it?
How can we get this done? There is something
you can smell in the black wing flap.
There is something warm in the neighbor's
kitchen light on through the shut window.
Do we belong in this?

**

I want to hear about the turnip's blood,
some ancient lockheed to the land I never
knew & what it gives you – words? Vague
pain that swells & yellows or collapses
& blackens down – red-giant pain – too much
gravity-memory. I want to make you
from what I know – grey cement
sidewalks and stiff blue air that numbs
your toes & makes you hard as itself then
lets you go. Tell me about the grass &
the birds on the water. Tell me
they let you go.

August 28th

My daughter: heave hungry & bent
waiting milky white in her velvet
underground sound adolescence.
My daughter: grown, weary
wandering leaflike down streets under
birds birdcalling in her voice but divorced
forgetting her mouth, her real teeth,
making her believe her own
disembodied sound.

I am watching what she is watching
A sort of daytime lurching,
the wind changing color.
We are fighting to be lookers
& not looked but hands come out
from all sides. We are zooed, foreign,
with price.

My daughter says it's your fault for dying
and mussing up the bed sheets. I'm so sorry.
I'm so so sorry but I'll keep it up –
hand over foot steepled to the bottle's lip
& keep changing each morning the bedding
in the boring impulse of shame.

My daughter is angry now that I am gone,
that I am gone-ing. My daughter is trying
to track my patterns in migratory flocks of sparrows
My daughter is trying to forget my name & good at it,
good for her. I gave her

my weak ankles and stitches that won't take
& it's been years out somewhere in this heat
where even the birds won't fly overhead.

Totem

Small circle box full of costume jewelry from the 1960's
& photos of my grandmother, a witch brooming,
demanding my mother clean the kitchen then flying
out the window,

and she did. With the shamed secrecy
of childhood putting on a record first:
Van Morrison Live in Belfast. My mother swing
dancing with the broom. Nothing ever got

clean. We left the last piece of fruit
in the basket until apple velcroed
to wicker. The whole house stuck to itself.
The mealy taste of Bartlett pears, my father
insisting they're good, not just on sale

like the fresh parsley stuck out of white
paper towels in the fridge we stopped buying
after she died, but this morning I used some

in my breakfast, cracking an egg over black
though today I can't tell how hungry I am
or if I believe I've got her eyes anymore. I decide I'll go
to the store, but waste time standing in the dumb
fluorescence fingering the pears just to remember
I remember one thing for sure.

View from the Corner of the Bar

A long plank of polished mahogany wood aged into a shit brown
that shines through scuffs & an impossibility of fingerprints

divided in the center by bronze taps going statue of liberty
green at the screws. One fizzing drop. Then lazy

another decides to follow into the trap below. Adjacent the stools stand –
at arms empty. Leaning forward, they tip to the bar's brown lip.

Along the east wall photos of forgotten little league teams,
those awkward boys aligned before a plastic skyblue so dull it greys.

They're smiling. Their fat coach crouches to their right hand side to match
their height, grinning with teeth.

Past their pale sea-foam uniforms, the window's a porthole
in the heavy door frame. Somewhere it is a blue bright day.

Light comes slanting in.
A small patch of the floor, black & white checkered,

is warmed. Once in a photo
my mother and father stand on some bar's identical floor.

My uncle's wedding. My mother's grasping my father's forearm
her dress palladium white. Tipsy

her face alight and looking up at his. Who looks directly to the camera, whiskey
raised to cheers. His tuxedo new. His face twenty years thinner, twenty

years cleaner. He is grinning,
a patch of sunlight plays at his feet.

How to Listen to a Bar Story

On the train to work, a boy with his corrugated mother & something's wrong
He's upset he keeps telling her bent over a little inside herself & every time
it quiets, starts again – It's not fair he keeps telling her. She closes
her book then says Well, I'll just have to listen to you more carefully
next time. That's all I can do.

It's not satisfying I can tell, but he rocks back and forth to wash it over
him stirring the milk into the coffee in his brain until it all goes white
& stops the sparking off. At work at the bar it's always like this: some drunk

father turned vagrant rambling & if I turn away long enough (I've perfected
the turn) it's always like this when I look back. That rocking. Small
circles maybe wanting to say no no no his head bobbing down at the neck
those tiny O's maybe saying it's okay yeah it's going to be –

Like the boy, is it fear alone in this impossible brain all misfiring inside & you
crosswired & unable to explain. You alone that big head those dumb memories
bouncing. If everything radiates some background vibration then that O cuts some air
shakes it. If I hand him bread & water to sober him up, I lean in close. I've spent years
bent this way praying to the space decided by that rhythm: let me in, let me listen.

Lleana

Her blonde hair perfected
down my shoulders

as my head snapped back
his push incendiary – Her like
this

like me but blue eyes water
& glass black pupil grown wide   When

she rolled out on blue
mats for naptime that big crystal

      eye open our secret – her head
      horizontal ship sailing off
      the edge of the flat world asking –
      am I asleep yet

My head snapped away the burn
his palm leaves Why is she not here

with me never here
was there no promise

More roman
candles than girls we weren't built
to last   I can't see her swan spark

anymore or know I remember right
that first time set going clean off &

for what
My head is our secret
Now our
bodies   let us find out where

they go

        how they bend and arc
          start to dissolve off from the center
once sent blind shaking
ascent into

Holy Poem

Sabbath dawning sea light. Tendrils coiling
the priest's hand drop down & bless
some ass, some girl nudging her mother's
calf but finds it unresponsive. She hides
in her Sunday dress but grows stalk-like,
sprouts up & is found out. A windmill
of time seems passing but is always just
then – the center of the spiral when she
was down there below waist-level in some
oak pew singing glory glory to the whale's
mouth that ate up Job or, no, the other
way round. Some spectacle of generosity
her mother's lord gave her to remember.
Puff down Jericho, munch the thousand loaves,
some water purpled and drunk. Sabbath's
dawning just right – starts the night
before – knelt bedside, mouth mouthing little
lies good to God, something about please &
thank you & fibs does not see herself dawning
sea light brighter than the priest's hand,
more holy than Sabbath. Let Job find his way,
wish him well. Her in her Sunday
dress is mouth of the whale, tongue,
and sated.

Apology for an Ending

after Robert Polito

When I can't make you understand I slide
back between your arms

grow small that way or go hold rocks
kick around stalagmites

along some pallid beach I can't ever really see.
You know?

I mean *really* see –
I stand there as long as I can bear

try to taste the salt misting off
the ocean, the white around the jetties foaming
a lone gull plunge, something dying then –

but it's all far off I can't see, I mean how I can taste
but when I bring

my mouth
to yours you don't –
the salt useless against my tongue

My tongue useless I slowly stop
returning your calls –

so quiet about it you won't know how
to fight it – if it's even happening

She seems distant –
you'll think I am –

but when I'm next to you barstools touching
or slid between last night and the morning
those moments the same

What will you do with me?

What will I do with you?

Where can we put each other now?

I shout up toward what I don't know
is distortion

Let my sparrow song crack when
it cannot sustain. Forgive me.

I'm young maybe
somewhere still inside myself. Stubborn I
just want you to see what I see to know how I can't

sometimes be right behind my eyes
and instead float between the black of my skull

How I can't choose this or how much I love you
or when it stops

What we can't do laps us years around
will I forget your cedar boned arms, your pulse

at my ear early morning and silent will I
dive nose first this ocean take up

residence with this impossible water
that horrible tide, forgive me,

now you know
I won't ask twice

The Fight

He's reaching across the table
palm up, fingers splayed
beneath her chin as if to say
like this, just like this, nothing
else. Tense bent knuckle giving
her a crude topography. See,
his hand falls down & rises,
levied before her face.
She keeps steady,
looking past him, her shoulders
drawn back, lips cinched,
palms flat pressed to the table top,
no interpretation between her body
and the veneer so she can be sure of it
like as a girl, lilting her fingers beneath the cold tap
water or cloying down into the black soil
for rocks, worms –
even now, the lip of her glass
as watching him speak absently
she wets her finger with her wine,
traces along the edge.
Makes it sing.

Acknowledgments

Thank you to all the lovely people at CAPS and Hayden Wayne for making this book a possibility. Thanks Emily and Michael for giving me a safe space to exist and encouraging me for as long as I can remember. I'd also like to thank Thomas Huggard for a meaningful kindness from a long time ago that still resonates. Thank you Mom if you can see this from wherever you might be for letting me know I could go. And thank you Joyce DeFilippo for being by my side in silence and (finally) in its absence.

Susan is receiving her MFA in poetry from Hunter College and her poems have appeared in *WayMark* and *I Want You to See This Before I Leave*. This is her first book.

Made in the USA
Las Vegas, NV
09 September 2021